YO-BWZ-564

THE

TUNED-IN,

TURNED-ON

BOOK

ABOUT LEARNING PROBLEMS

by Marnell L. Hayes

Academic Therapy Publications
Novato, California

Academic Therapy Publications
20 Commercial Boulevard
Novato, California 94949-6191

Library of Congress Catalog Card Number: 74-80091

International Standard Book Number: 0-87879-090-X

9 8 7 6 5 4 3 2 1 0
4 3 2 1 0 9 8 7 6 5

Table of Contents

It's More Than An Introduction

"I'm glad to write this because I think anybody like me would like this book.

"I used alot of the visual Handy-Dandy Hints. It helps me alot.

"This book is good for any age person. I use the hints everyday. Maybe even 5 or 6 times a day.

"My learning dissability is learning with my ears. I can't learn with my ears but I'm a good visual learner. I have to listen very carfully to what anybody says and use my eyes as much as possible so I can know and remember what they say.

"But you'll have to understand if the author sounds like a mother sometimes its only because She *is* one. She's my mom."

Valli Hayes (age 12)
Junior Editorial Consultant

Introduction

This book is for kids (though I'd be pleased and proud if their parents and teachers read it, too). I've tried to write it so that it's interesting to read, and not *too* "preachy." My twelve-year-old daughter, one of the best visual learners I know (and, as she herself admits, one of the *poorest* auditory learners), has carefully edited my work, taking out as many "icky" parts as she could. I found her suggestions invariably useful, and her work contributed greatly to the manuscript.

Parts of the book have also been checked over by some other young people I know, including a young lady who's just beginning to read (so her mother reads the chapters to her), a boy who has just gone from a special learning disability class to a regular class, and a very bright young woman who had serious learning problems all through school, whose encouragement provided the final spurt of energy I needed to finish the book.

The ideas you'll find here came from many, many sources—some have become so much a part of me and my own learning processes that I can't remember *not* using them. Some came from teachers. But, not too strangely, most of the ideas came from kids.

Parents will want to read this book before, after, or with their children—preferably all three! Tapes of the text are available for nonreaders, those whose reading needs a "boost," and for group counseling or classroom use.*

Anybody who reads this book will think of a dozen ideas I might have used, but didn't. That's good! When our ideas start multiplying, we're really on the right track. I'd love to hear some other crazy or strange learning and study ideas, especially ones from you kids. You can tell me how the book helped you, too.

"Dr. H."

Dr. Marnell L. Hayes
Department of Special Education
Texas Woman's University
Denton, TX   76204

---

*The ninety-minute cassette tape recording of the book is available from the publisher for $7.95.

To Valli, with special thanks;
To Roberta, who'll write her own book someday;
To Janie, who can swim a mile and throw a marshmallow;

> *and to Dougie,*
> *and Michelle,*
> *and Jeff,*
> *and Cheri,*
> *and Mike,*
> *and Brenda-bear,*
> *and Bonnie,*
> *and Chantelle,*
> *and Susan,*
> *and Philbert,*
> *and Shannon,*

and to all the other kids who've taught me, and who *will* teach me,
This little book is dedicated with love.

Chapter 1

"Who Are You, And Why Are You Writing This Book?"

I'm a college professor. I'm in the business of teaching teachers how to teach. That surprises many kids, because it seems like teachers were just always teachers. Sometimes you don't realize that they had to *learn* to teach, and it was pretty hard for some of them! You should see me grade their papers. Sometimes I have to promise them not to tell their students what their grades are!

I also work with kids sometimes. I help to find out why they have trouble learning. I want to know what things are hard for them, and what things they do well. Then I try to help their teachers and parents decide what kinds of things will help them learn better. If there's nobody who *can* help, then I try to let the kids themselves know the best ways for them to learn.

Kids teach *me*, too. One thing they have taught me is that, sometimes, no one can help you as much as you can help yourself. After all, no matter how much your parents care, or your teachers, nobody cares as much as you do yourself—because it's *your* life, right?

I'm writing this book because I think kids want to know more about their problems. Sometimes you worry a whole lot more when you don't know what's wrong, or what's going to happen, or what to do about it.

The problem is that sometimes adults think kids are too young to know about things like money problems, or sickness, or family problems, or even their own school problems! So you worry. You know something is wrong, and sometimes the things you think it might be are worse than what it really is!

I have another reason for writing this book, too. I have a daughter who can use the information I am going to write for you. She needs to have it written down, because that's the way she learns best. She is going to help me with this book. She will read the chapters as I write them, so that she can tell me if I am saying things in a way that kids (the little guys, the pre-teenagers like she is, and the teenagers) will be able to use them.

Now a question for you: Why are you reading this book?

Most likely, somebody gave you the book to read. Maybe it was your teacher, or one of your parents, or your doctor or counselor. Somebody thought that you were old enough, and— let's face it—*smart* enough to know what's going on.

You must be having some trouble in school. That *is* what this book is about, after all. Maybe reading is your problem. Or maybe it's math. Whatever it is, if I know kids, you have been trying to figure out why something that's easy for your friends is hard for you. It doesn't seem fair, right?

Maybe you've already put a lot of thought into that. Maybe you think you've figured out what's wrong.

Maybe you've decided that you're dumb, and nobody wants to hurt your feelings, so they're not telling you.

That's the first thing I can clear up for you.

Dumb, you're not. If you were dumb nobody would have told you to read this book. As a matter of fact, you wouldn't be able to understand the ideas in this book. Later, I'll explain more about why I know you're not dumb. But right now, let's get on with the business of finding out what *is* wrong.

The person who told you to read this book may have already told you what the problem is. If not, here it is: Your problem is what we call a learning disability, or LD for short. What that means is that basically, you're a pretty smart kid—at least average, and maybe even smarter—but that you have problems learning some kinds of things. You're not dumb; that would mean that you would have trouble learning *everything.* And you know that's not you!

You may be interested to know that some pretty famous people may have had learning disabilities. Did you know that Albert Einstein had a lot of trouble in school, especially with math? And the great Leonardo daVinci was a "mirror writer"—he wrote backwards as well as he wrote forwards! And nobody, *but nobody,* could call them dumb.

So a learning disability is a pretty far cry from being dumb, because part of the definition says that you have to be as smart as the average, or smarter! This book is to tell you more about what we mean by learning disability, and that's what the next chapter will do. Then there is a chapter that will give you some good ideas for studying, and some neat tricks to show your parents and teachers why some things are hard for you. The last part of the book has some ideas for homework you can assign to your parents and teachers (after all, that's only fair)!

Chapter 2

"What's A Learning Disability, Or If I'm So Smart, Why Do I Have Trouble Learning?"

One of the problems in talking about learning disabilities is that even the "experts" have trouble explaining it to each other!

Let's start with what you already know.

Some kids just don't have trouble learning anything. (Lucky!) They're good readers, good writers, good in math, spelling—everything. That's not you.

Some kids *do* have trouble learning—with everything from talking and walking to reading and math. Some kids have so much trouble learning that they may not even be in school, or may have to have special help even for dressing. That's pretty tough; but that's not you, either.

Kids like you are a real whiz at some things. And some things are just impossible. Let me tell you about some kids with learning disabilities that I've known.

1. Cathy was six, and in the first grade. She could read anything—even sixth-grade books. But she had trouble sitting still and remembering anything her teacher told her.

2. Chuck was thirteen. He was a good reader, too, and pretty fair in math—but he couldn't even write one sentence. He could follow complicated repair books written for adults, though, to take apart his motor bike and put it together again.

3. Beth was twenty. She was smarter than some of her teachers, but the counselor at her college thought she shouldn't even be there. Beth had a speech problem, but her learning problem was the biggest trouble: Whenever she tried to write, some of the words would "get lost" before she could get them on paper.

4. Billy was eleven, and a real "brain" in math. But he couldn't read a first-grade book.

5. Jeff was twelve. He was both a good baseball player, and good in reading and math. But he was always in trouble because he didn't even seem to notice when the teacher called on him! Sometimes he fooled around a lot in class, too.

Maybe one of these kids sounds a lot like you. Maybe not. The thing you probably noticed was that they all had some good points, and some bad ones. Just like you.

For a long time, the experts didn't even know there *was* such a thing as a learning disability. They knew there were kids like you, who were plenty smart but who had trouble learning. They thought the problem was one of these things you've probably heard before:

"He doesn't try!"

"She could do it if she'd put her mind to it."

"There's no discipline at home!"

"It's the parents' fault."

"It's the school's fault."

"It's the kid's fault!"

"If they'd cut out the TV and make him study, he could do it."

"She isn't motivated."

"He just doesn't care."

"If he'd behave himself he could learn!"

Sound familiar?

Finally the experts began to see that kids like you *did* try. (Sure, sometimes when you found out how tough it was, you gave up and pretended you didn't care—but that was after you *really* tried, and somebody wrote in red on your paper, "Why don't you try?" But you always cared, deep down.)

The experts began to see patterns in the way you learned and didn't learn. At last they came up with that name for the problem: Learning Disability.

The only problem then was that they explained it several different ways. Here are some of the things most of the experts seem to agree on:

First, they all seem to agree that you've got to be average or better in "smarts" to "qualify" for a learning disability!

Some experts noticed that kids like you do very poorly in some areas, and very well in others (like my young friends I described to you earlier). We can show this on a chart, for an imaginary student named Bill:

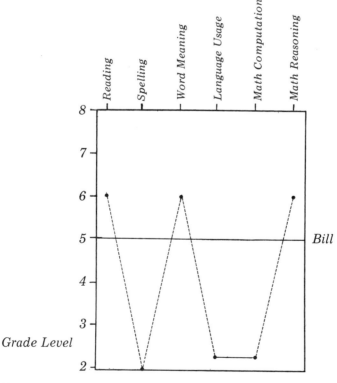

What this shows is that Bill is a fifth grader. He's a great reader—he reads like a sixth grader. But he doesn't spell any better than a second grader. He knows a lot of words, but his grammar is terrible. He's a sloppy math student, and makes a lot of errors; but he really understands what he's supposed to be doing in those "story" problems.

All of this makes the dotted line on Bill's chart go up and down sharply, instead of along an even line at his grade level. We call it a "jagged profile." That's probably pretty much what your profile would look like, too, but maybe not in the same subjects.

A report card for Bill might show the same sort of thing—some good grades and some really terrible ones. The older Bill gets, the more likely all of those grades are to be low if somebody doesn't figure out what's wrong and lend a hand. If you're in the sixth or seventh grade (or above) and you don't read well, for example, you know you will run into trouble in social studies if the teacher wants you to do much reading.

Sometimes a learning disability is even more basic than a problem in reading or math. Often, a learning disability can mean having problems with anything you have to learn by *seeing.* For some who may learn well with their eyes, it can be problems in learning what they *hear.*

This doesn't mean that the person needs glasses or a hearing aid. These students may have "20-20" vision or perfect hearing. It's just that what they learn with the problem gets mixed up or too quickly forgotten.

What causes learning disabilities?

Don't we wish we knew! We are pretty sure that it has something to do with the ways in which our brains work, but we can't be sure just what.

For a while, most of the experts thought that learning disabilities were caused by damage or injury to the brain. That was because people (usually adults, like soldiers who had been hurt in battle) had learning problems and sometimes behavior problems that looked a lot like the learning problems and behavior problems that some children and teenagers had.

That idea made sense to a lot of people. Parents of a child with a learning problem would think back and remember a time when their child fell out of his high chair, or down the stairs, or off a tricycle. They thought that perhaps his brain had been damaged then.

The problem is, just about nobody can think of a child who *didn't* fall out of his high chair, or down the stairs, or off his tricycle!

The doctors would often do a type of medical test called an EEG, in which little wires are attached to the patient's head with a kind of jelly, and the brain waves are traced. (You may have had one of these tests—remember how hard it was to wash the goo out of your hair?)

Very often, the EEG would be perfectly normal. And sometimes, when they would check people who learned well, they found tracings that were *not* normal! So that didn't always give any answers.

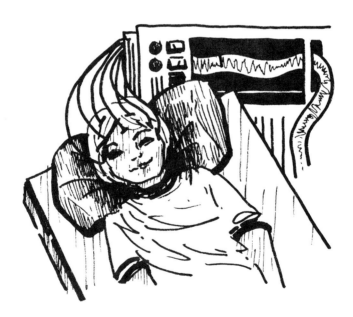

The experts finally decided that we couldn't really blame the problem on brain damage unless we knew there really was some damage—and the doctors couldn't very well open your head and take a look. Besides, "brain damage" sounds pretty scary and really doesn't tell what kind of trouble you're having.

Even though we don't know for sure what *does* cause learning disability, there are a lot of things we're pretty sure do not cause it.

I have already told you that having a learning disability does not mean being "dumb" or retarded. We also know that poor eyesight or bad hearing are not causes of a learning disability. A learning disability is not caused by emotional problems—even though the kinds of problems you run into with a learning disability can cause you to feel pretty emotional sometimes, as I'm sure you know!

We have a pretty good idea that the problem *is* within the brain, though we don't know where, how, or why. What we *do* know is that your brain works pretty well in most ways, or you wouldn't be as smart as you are.

That gives you a pretty good idea of what a learning disability is, but let me sum it up:

A learning disability is a problem in one or more areas of learning. It can be in a specific school subject, like math, reading, or language. It can be in a whole learning area, such as problems in learning things through seeing them or hearing them. While we may not know the cause, we know that it is *not* mental retardation, poor eyesight, bad hearing, or emotional problems.

Now let's find out how to find out more about your own special problems, OK?

Chapter 3

"So How Do I Dig Out The Truth About Myself?"

By now you've figured out that if you're going to help yourself, you're going to need information. But where do you get this information?

Here are some of the people who may have information you can use:

> Your teacher
> Your parents
> Your family doctor
> Your school counselor

It may turn out that none of them has *all* of the information you need. Your teacher will know how you are doing in class, and your parents will know a lot (maybe too much!) about your behavior. Your doctor, and probably your parents, too, will know how healthy you are. Your school counselor or your teacher may be the only one who knows how you did on those tests you took at school.

You may have to do some detective work to get the information you need. I will give you some of the questions you need to ask, and maybe that will help. You may know some of the answers to these questions yourself, without asking anyone else.

1. What do my teachers think is my biggest all around problem in school?

2. What's my very worst school subject?

3. What's my best school subject?

4. Have my eyes been checked lately?Were they OK?(If not, tell your folks to "get with it.")

5. Have I had a hearing test lately?How did it come out? (Again–if not, talk to your folks. They can probably get the school to give you one.)

6. Have I had a check-up with the doctor recently? Am I pretty healthy, and am I getting enough sleep, and drinking plenty of milk, and all that other good stuff?(This is another must. To get the most from your body and brain, you've got to keep them in good working order, like a fine Italian ten-speed bike, or a hot little sports car.)

7. In what school subjects am I below grade level?

8. In what subjects am I doing grade-level work or better? If I'm not doing grade level work in any subjects, what *seems* to be preventing me (since I am average or smarter) from doing grade level work or better?

    a. Is it my reading ability?

    b. Is it my spelling?

    c. Is it my writing?

    d. Could it be my listening skills?

    e. Is it my memory?

    f. How about my behavior?

    g. Or is it something else?

Now let's try to see if we can get even more information. Let's try to get right at the root of things, and find out where the real problem is, and what's the best way for you to learn. That will help you find the best way to solve the problem you found in Number 8 above.

Here are two lists. Look them over, and check the things that seem to describe *you* best. You can get your parents or your teacher to check them, too, without looking at your answers. Then count up your check-marks and see which list describes you best.

List A

___ 1. People say you have *terrible* handwriting.

___ 2. You don't like silent filmstrips, pantomimes, or charades.

___ 3. You'd rather do a music activity than art; and you'd rather listen to a tape than look at a filmstrip.

___ 4. Your teacher says you leave out words, or sometimes you get words or letters backwards.

___ 5. You can spell better out loud than when you have to write it down.

___ 6. You remember things you talk about in class much better than stuff you have to read.

___ 7. You don't copy from the board very well.

___ 8. You like jokes or riddles better than cartoons or crossword puzzles.

___ 9. You like games with a lot of action or noise better than checkers or most other board games.

___ 10. You understand better when you read aloud.

___ 11. Sometimes you mess up in math because you don't notice the sign or because you read the numbers or directions wrong.

___ 12. You're the last one to notice something new—that the classroom was painted, or that there's a new bulletin board display.

___ 13. Map activities are just not your "thing"—you never can seem to remember what continent Chile is in, or if Nebraska is north, east, south, or west of Missouri.

___ 14. You often get in trouble for "sloppy work," even on workbook pages.

___ 15. You use your finger as a "pointer" when you read, but you still get lost and skip words or lines sometimes.

___ 16. Sometimes you get in trouble for humming or whistling to yourself when you're working.

___ 17. Sometimes your eyes just "bother" you; but your eye tests come out OK, or you've already got glasses that the eye doctor says are just right for you.

___ 18. You hate "ditto" sheet activities (those purple-printed sheets) especially blotty ones. They're tough for you.

___ 19. "Matching" test questions, where you have to draw lines to the right answer, or you have to fill in the letters in order, are a real problem.

___ 20. Sometimes when you read, you mix up words that look almost alike, like *pull* and *pill* or *bale* and *dale*.

_____ *Score*

The Auditory Learner

List V

____ 1. It seems like you're always having to ask somebody to repeat what he just said.

____ 2. Sometimes you find yourself "tuned out" in class—staring out the window, maybe, when you were really trying to pay attention.

____ 3. Often you know what you want to say, but you just can't think of the word. Sometimes you may even be accused of "talking with your hands," or calling something a "thingamajig" or "whatcha-callit."

____ 4. You may be in speech therapy, or may have been at some time before.

____ 5. You have trouble understanding the teacher sometimes when her back is turned so you can't see her face while she's talking.

____ 6. It's usually easier to look and see what everybody else is doing than to try to get the teacher to repeat the instructions.

____ 7. When you watch TV or play records, somebody is always yelling "Turn that thing down!"

____ 8. Your parents or teachers say you say "Huh?" too much.

____ 9. You'd rather demonstrate how to do something than make a speech.

____ 10. Words that sound almost alike (like *bill* and *bell* or *pin* and *pen*) give you a lot of trouble. Sometimes you can't tell them apart.

____ 11. You have trouble remembering your homework assignment unless your teacher writes it on the board or you write it down.

____ 12. You like board games like checkers better than listening games.

____ 13. Sometimes you make mistakes in speaking (like saying "He got *expended* from school") that everybody but you thinks are funny.

____ 14. You have to go over most of the alphabet to remember whether *M* comes before or after *R*, and so forth.

____ 15. You like art work better than music activities.

____ 16. You do better when the teacher *shows* you what to do, not just *tells* you.

____ 17. You can do lots of things that are hard to explain with words—like fixing your bike or doing macramé.

____ 18. People are always telling you to "answer in a complete sentence" because you usually answer questions with just "yes" or "no."

____ 19. Often you forget to give messages to people—when someone calls on the telephone for one of your parents, for example.

____ 20. You're always drawing little pictures on the edges of your papers, or "doodling" on scratch paper.

_____ *Score*

The Visual Learner

Now let's look at your scores. Which is higher?

If List A is very much higher than List V, it gives us hints that your problems are in learning with your *eyes*, and your best way of learning is with your *ears*. We might call you an auditory learner. If your teacher or counselor agrees that the items you checked describe you pretty well, then skip ahead to Chapter 4, Section A. It will give you some study helps that work best for auditory learners like you.

If your List V score was much higher, then you tend to have problems learning with your ears. Your eyes will be your best keys to learning. You could be called a visual learner. You don't even have to read Section A of Chapter 4. Just skip right ahead to Section V. It's tailor-made for visual learners.

And what happens if both scores are pretty close to one another? Well, if you have trouble in learning with your eyes and with your ears, then you'll need all the help you can get to get that average-or-better brain going! We can use some special aids to learning by *touching* and *doing.* Chapter 5 is for you, and it has some hints your parents and teachers won't believe!

Now, there's one more thing we can do to be sure we've got your problem figured out right. If you have already had a lot of special tests, either in school or at a special clinic, you may be able to get your teacher or your parents to find out if those tests gave information that agrees with what we have found in our check lists. If that information does *not* agree with the check list, then go over the check list again. If it *still* doesn't agree, then it might be a good idea to go along with the "experts." Try the section of the next chapter that goes along with what the tests found. If that doesn't help, well, then we'll go along with your very own opinions and our check list!

Let's get with it.

Chapter 4

"How Do I Beat The Rap And Avoid Pain In Studying?"

First of all, if you cheated and didn't read Chapter 3, you'd better go back! Only one part of this chapter is really for you, and Chapter 3 tells you how to figure out which part it is.

Second, this chapter isn't going to try to "cure" your learning problem. That's a pretty tall order, and takes a lot more information than you and I can dig out without meeting face-to-face! Besides, your classroom teacher, counselor, or maybe a resource teacher is probably already working on remedial activities to improve those things you're having the most trouble with.

What this chapter *will* do is to help you make the most of the things you do *best*. It will give you some ideas for studying that will help you learn the most as easily and quickly as possible.

So pick out the section for your "learning style" and see what suggestions you can use.

Section 4-A

*Super-Special Suggestions for Auditory Learners
(And for Auditory Learners Only!
Visual Learners go to the next section.)*

The first thing to remember is to tune in on voices! You already know that you learn more from school lessons that were talked about in class. Why not use your *own* voice as a study aid, too?

It's even easier than it sounds. You just do all the studying you can, right out loud! Here's how you can use this idea in some different school subjects:

Reading

If you're having trouble in reading, ask if your reading teacher is using one of the "phonics" approaches. (That means using the sounds of letters and groups of letters to figure out the words.) That's the way *you'll* learn to read best.

If you have stories or poems to read for school, you'll understand them and remember them best if you read them out loud. If there isn't a quiet corner in your classroom where you can read, get permission to take the books home. You can sit in your room, or outside, and read aloud. Reading close into a corner may even help bounce the sound back into your ears better, and may help you keep your mind on your reading. Your ears will do the rest!

If you're really a pretty "crummy" reader, see if you can get someone to read the material to you while you follow along. Or, if you're lucky enough to own (or borrow) a tape recorder, get someone to tape the material for you.

A really good skill for you to work on is saying the words "inside your head" silently. If you practice this enough, it works as well as reading aloud. A good thing about this is that you can even do it in the library, where you *can't* talk out loud!

I'm sure you've already noticed that when your teacher has you read silently in class, she has told you "I said, 'silently'!" or "I see some people moving their lips!" Well, the fact is, you were reading not-quite-silently because your brain "knew" you needed to hear the words to learn them best. The reason your teacher tried to get you to *stop* whispering the words or moving your lips is because she knows that people read more slowly that way. When you read aloud, you can't read faster than you can talk! But what your teacher didn't know, maybe, was that some people really *need* to say all the words. For you, or for anybody else, it is better to read slowly and *learn* than to speed along if you can't remember what you read—right?

Writing

Here's where that "talking to yourself" can come in handy again. If you often leave out letters or words, try it this way:

1. Plan the sentence you want to write by saying it out loud or silently.

2. Say it over two or three times until you're sure you've got it just the way you want it.

3. Then write it while you say it slowly.

If you're copying something, just:

1. Read it over.

2. Then close your eyes and repeat it to yourself until you've got it.

3. Then just write it out, saying it once more, slowly.

If you are in junior high or high school, and if you have to write a lot of papers, you can use a tape recorder as a special help. You can dictate each sentence as you plan it. Then you can play it back to make changes, and finally, play it back one sentence at a time as you write it down.

If you have learned to type, you'll be much better at making up your own stories or term papers right at the typewriter than many visual learners!

Spelling

Writing the words five times each is not a good way for you to study! Instead:

1. Say the word while you look at it. Then say each letter aloud. (Keep your finger on the word so you won't lose your place. Say it this way: "Book, b-o-o-k, book.")

2. Close your eyes and say and spell it again. Then open your eyes and check it.

3. Now close your eyes and say and spell it one more time.

4. Last, open your eyes and write the word, writing the letters by trying to hear them over again in your mind. Then check it. If you get it wrong, *mark it out* or erase it so you can't see it, and go through the steps again.

Now that you've studied the words, you can have someone call them out to you. Remember to "hear" the spelling of the word in your head before you start to write! This is the way to do it when you have a spelling test, too.

Math

Those flash cards teachers like to use for math may not help you, unless you find a way to turn them into signals your ears can use! Try it this way, with only three or four cards at a time:

1. First, look at the flash card on the answer side. (For example, let's say the problem is 3 x 2 = 6.) Read the whole thing aloud.
2. Then close your eyes and recite it several times.
3. Next, go on to the next two or three cards, doing the same thing. (Be sure you don't try to work on too many at one time.)
4. Then turn the cards over to the side without the answers. Read the problem out loud and try to "hear" the answer, then say it.
5. Turn the card over, and check it. If you didn't get the right answer, fix it quickly by reading the whole thing, problem and answer, over several times.

You will find some other math hints that you can use if you have trouble learning your times tables, in Chapter 5.

Whenever you have trouble with math homework, try working the problem by explaining it to yourself, out loud. Because of the way you learn best, you will often find your mistakes with your ears, as soon as you hear them, even if your eyes have gone over the problem again and again.

Other School Subjects

Talk, talk, talk! *Listen* to yourself talk about all your school subjects. If you have to study a map, go over it, and **tell yourself** all about it, sort of like this:

"Well, I see Florida down there, looking kinda like a thumb. That great big one over there is Texas. And up here, separate from the others, is Alaska . . . ," and so on.

You can do this with other subjects, too. If you're a good reader, just read it out loud and listen to yourself. You can read from the book, or from notes, or a study outline. If you're *not* a good reader, you can get someone to read to you, or a parent or friend to help you study by talking to you about the subject. It doesn't matter whether it's history, science, or health. Just "talk it up."

A fun way to study that works well if you have to learn lists of things is to make up silly words, called *acronyms*, where each letter stands for the first letter of the things you have to remember. You can also make silly sentences, with each word beginning with the same letter as the word you have to remember. Even some chemists and mathemeticians use acronyms to help them remember certain formulas or numbers!

Another way is to make up "cheers," like school cheers: "Petals! Sepals! Pistil! Stamen! Yea-a-a-a-a, FLOWER!" It's silly, but it works.

You probably learned the alphabet with the aid of the "Alphabet Song," or used the "Thirty Days Hath September" song to help you figure out whether May has 30 or 31 days. There are many such useful poems and songs for helping people remember anything from the digits after the decimal point for the number that represents *pi* [π], or the kings of England. And you'd be surprised how many teachers and professors use these little tricks to help them remember!

You can think up many more ideas to use your own voice and your ears to help you learn. It doesn't have to be hard, serious work all the time. And by the way, if some of your friends think some of these study helps are weird, just you wait. Pretty soon they'll be using your ideas, too!

Now skip ahead to Chapter 5 for some crazy ideas you won't believe until you've tried them!

Section 4–V

Handy-Dandy Hints for Visual Learners
(And for Visual Learners Only!
Auditory Learners should go back and read Section A.
If you've already read it, then skip ahead to Chapter 5.)

Look and learn—that's your byword. You'll need to use your eyes for your best learning. You already know that what you've seen, you're more likely to remember. When you see a film you're the one who remembers all the details—maybe, sometimes, even better than your teacher!

Your secret weapon will be learning how to make "mind pictures" out of things you see and hear. And it's easier than it sounds. You already know how to do it; you just have to do it more. For example, if somebody says "butterfly," many of your classmates just hear the word. But you *see* a butterfly, in "living color" in your mind's eye!

You may even be surprised that some people *can't* do this. They can't even imagine how their bedroom would look with a shaggy red bedspread and blue pennants on the wall, or whether a silver glitter helmet will look great or awful with a green 'cycle.

You can use your ability to "see" and imagine. Just turn the spoken words your teacher uses into pictures! Let's see how this works with different school subjects.

Reading

The kind of reading approach that's best for you would be a "look-and-say" approach. If you're still a beginning reader, you or your parents may want to talk to your teacher and find out what kind of method she's using. If it's a "phonics" method, woe is you! Perhaps your parents or school counselor can talk to your teacher about this. There are many good methods for teaching reading which use the *eyes* more than the ears—and that's for you.

Sight words, flash cards, and experience stories will be things your teacher will use. If you're already reading, but are getting help to be a better reader, you will do better if you *don't* try to "sound out" new words. Instead, look at the word. Does it look like some of the "sight" words you already know? After you've figured out what word it *looks* like, then you can try to figure out what sounds are different. This means that looking at the whole word comes first. Then you may only have to sound out one or two letters, not all of them!

Writing

You may need to go over anything you write, more than once. You'll probably leave out a word or two, or do some weird spelling, because most people make up things they want to write by "hearing" them in their minds first—and learning by hearing just isn't your thing.

One way to catch your mistakes before the teacher does, is to write what authors call a "rough draft." This is a messy copy that you will correct and rewrite. Skip lines! That way you have plenty of room to fit in whatever you might leave out. After you've written your rough draft, and checked over it for errors or better ways to say things, then recopy it. You'll make fewer errors if you use a sheet of paper or ruler as a guide under each line of your rough draft as you copy it. That way you won't get lost and end up copying the wrong line.

Writing a rough draft first *does* take more time. That means you have to be a good planner, so you won't run out of time! This isn't so important for homework, term papers, or book reports. But when you only have a certain amount of time, like on a test, you can't waste *any* time when you know you're going to have to copy your paper over. A good way to be sure you write everything you want to say without wasting too much time is to make a very quick outline, right on the margin of your paper. It doesn't have to be fancy—just enough to remind you of the points you want to make, like this:

GENERAL CUSTER
1. His record
2. His temper and vanity
3. Little Big Horn
   A. Custer's mistakes
   B. Number killed
   C. What happened later

What happens if you run out of time, and you haven't finished recopying your answer? First, ask the teacher to give you more time. If that's not possible, then turn in what you have—rough draft, outline, and all. Your teacher can see that you had a good answer, and may give credit, even if he or she has to wade through your rough draft to find it!

Copying from the board or a book is easy for you, if you do it this way:

1. Look at the whole word or sentence.

2. Close your eyes, and try to "see" the picture of it in your mind, just as it was written.

3. Then, instead of looking back and forth from the board to your paper, you just copy it from the picture in your mind!

With practice, you can get good at this—and it's something only visual learners, like you, *can* do well.

Spelling

You've got to "see" the words to spell them. Study new words with your eyes, looking at them first, then closing your eyes and making a "picture" of the word in your mind. Then just read the letters from the "picture"! Using this method, visual learners make excellent spellers!

Another good way to work on spelling—*after* you've done plenty of that "picture making"—is to write each word a few times. Look at the word, see it in your mind's eye, and write it. Check it and then copy it once or twice.

If someone wants to call the words out to you, or if your teacher has spelling bees, do it this way: When the word is called, close your eyes and try to picture it. Then just read the letters off the picture. It'll work!

Math

Flash cards were practically invented for you! Use them to study math combinations, or, if you're a high school student, to study formulas.

Let's use easy math combinations as an example of how visual learners should use flash cards.

First, your flash card should have two sides—one side with the problem, and one side with the problem and the answer (not just the answer!). Look at the problem side. If you know the answer, say it, and try to "see" it in the blank. Then turn the card over and check it. If you were wrong, run your eyes over the problem and correct answer several times.

When you have *new* math combinations or formulas to learn, start with the side with the answer! Look across the problem and answer. Then turn the card over and try to "see" the answer in the blank. Turn back to the answer side and check.

For "story" problems, try to "visualize" all the items. If it says, "Three boys each have four apples . . . ," imagine those boys and those apples. It'll help! You can also make little sketches on scratch paper as you're working problems.

Other School Subjects

Look at everything. Use your eyes constantly. Look at pictures, maps and charts. If you can learn to make *very short* outlines for things you have to study, you can look them over just before tests.

Acronyms are good study helps, too. An acronym is a word made up of the first letters of several words. It's easier to say

UNICEF than United Nations International Children's Emergency Fund, right? If you need to remember a list of things, make up a silly acronym. It doesn't even have to form a word. Couldn't you remember Truman-Eisenhower-Kennedy-Johnson-Nixon better if you had made a mind's-eye picture of TEKJN?

You can use color to help you learn, too. Visual learners often find that making colored notes, or even underlining in color, can help boost those mental pictures. Auditory learners can use tape recorders, which are expensive. You can do better and cheaper as a visual learner by stocking up on all sorts of paper—some white, some lined, some colored; some in a variety of notebooks, some not—and lots of those marvelous fine-point felt-tip pens in many colors. You'll want a few transparent underliners, perhaps; some regular wide markers; and large heavy cards for flash cards—and a knapsack to carry all this junk in!

Be sure to give yourself all the visual help you can. Make lists! Write notes to yourself! Write down your homework assignments—that's better than not being able to remember what you had to do. Also, get your parents in the note-writing habit. The best place for their reminders to you (or messages to them) is probably where they go at our house—right on the refrigerator door. That's one place none of us snacksters will miss.

It's a good idea to keep a little note pad with you all the time at school. Then you're set to make notes before you forget— whether it's about your homework or a reminder for your parents about PTA.

If you're in junior high or high school and you have under-standing teachers, you can ask them to look over the notes you take in class. You may miss some of the things you heard, but if they help you get them in your notes so your eyes can work on them, you've got it made.

Remember—your eyes can do your learning for you, but only if you provide the right things for them to see.

Now skip ahead to Chapter 5 for some strange study ideas. Some may be just right for you!

43

Chapter 5

Crazy Ideas For Everybody

Not all of these hints will be just right for you. Some will be solutions to problems you don't even have! Try out some of the crazy study hints, though; and at least take a good look at some of the other ideas. There just may be a suggestion you can use!

Here's one nobody believes—at least, not until they've tried it. It's a counting-on-your-fingers method for doing multiplication.

First, chances are you've been counting on your fingers for math all along—but you may have had to do it under your desk because your teacher didn't approve. I'd better explain that I *do* approve of counting on your fingers—I couldn't add or subtract if I didn't!

Now, here's how this method works. (You'll have to put this book down and really *do* it to learn it.) This works for any multiplication combination from 6 through 10. (You won't need the 10's though. They're easy!) You'll have to learn up through the 5's the "old" way.

Make fists and stick up both thumbs. You'll just have to remember that "Thumbs are 6's."

Now we'll do 7 x 8. We count up each number we want to multiply, one on each hand, starting on either hand by sticking out fingers, remembering that thumbs are 6's:

Now some of your fingers are sticking out and some are curled in. Count the sticking-out ones by 10's (10-20-30-40-50), and you get 50.

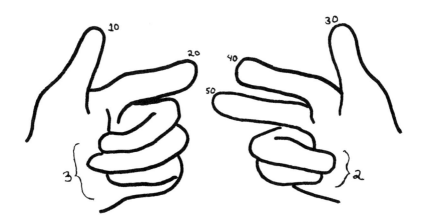

Now count the turned-in ones on each hand (3 on one hand, 2 on the other), and multiply these two little numbers:

$$2 \times 3 = 6$$

Now add the 50 and the 6, and your answer is 56.

Neat trick, eh?

Now, you may be thinking that that's a pretty complicated thing to learn. It is—but if you have trouble memorizing the times tables, this is well worth the trouble! (To tell the truth, I use it all the time. I never *can* seem to remember 8 x 9 or 9 x 7.)

If you still aren't sure of that one, try some other problems until you're sure you've got it. Then teach it to someone else—that's the best way to learn something. Teach it to your math teacher for a special treat. Maybe if you do, he or she will understand that counting on fingers is OK after all!

Another crazy trick is studying with rhythm. Maybe you already do this sometimes. Many people find counting on their fingers easier if they tap each finger as they count it (me, too!). Some even work best if they tap a certain way, like on the ends of their noses!

If you have things to memorize, foot tapping or hand clapping might just help. You can tap the desk top, drum-fashion, as you recite the material you have to learn. Auditory learners seem to learn from the *sound* of the tapping; perhaps the visual learners learn from *seeing* and *doing*!

Both the finger-counting and rhythm learning methods are bound to raise some eyebrows. If you go all out on the tapping and thumping while studying in your room, you may have a tall bit of explaining to do to your parents!

Another good method that some auditory and visual learners both find useful is "finger writing on texture." You've probably seen and used sandpaper letters, which you trace with a fingertip to help you remember how it *feels* to form a certain letter. Perhaps you even learned to write this way. If it worked then, why not use it now? You can practice "writing" with a fingertip on any rough surface, and the action you use in forming the word may help you remember it. This book's "junior editorial consultant" finds that writing on a blue-jeaned knee works well, especially when she doesn't have pencil and paper handy for her visual learning style. Mrs. Polly Behrmann suggests getting one of those old blue-gray canvas-colored notebooks. They're not as pretty as the slick, full-color ecology notebooks—but that scratchy canvas is just the thing for finger writing. (You'll find some of Mrs. Behrmann's books, full of learning games and ideas, listed in the last chapter.)

Now for some ideas to help solve special problems.

One of the biggest problems with a learning disability is that it isn't just *one* problem. You may have trouble with math, but be a good reader. Someone else may be just the opposite. And besides all that, there are some problems other than learning problems that some (but not all) kids with learning disabilities have. Maybe it's just another way of proving that no two people are exactly alike!

We do need to look at some of the problems that aren't directly connected to learning, and look for some solutions.

One of the problems that many kids with learning disabilities have is really a group of problems. They're sometimes called "short attention span" or maybe "distractibility"; and they're sometimes related to "hyperactivity." This means that your attention span hops from one thing to another too much, and that doing one thing for very long (especially holding still!) is tough for you. You probably move around and fidget a lot, too.

How do you know if you've got trouble with this? Easy! If you often wondered how the other kids in your class can work so long on one assignment, or if somebody's always asking "Can't you *sit still?*" Or if, when you're trying to work on something, you often find yourself looking at, listening to, or fiddling with something else. Well, maybe you've got a touch of one or all of this group of problems!

How do you deal with this? Here are some things to try.

First, it's true—you *will* be able to learn better if you clear off and clean off your desk first. If all those books, pencils, scratch pads, and the assorted junk isn't right in front of you, it can't distract you. So clear it up.

Don't over-do, though! Sometimes when I have work I *really* am putting off, I spend as much time as I can tidying my desk and sharpening all my pencils three or four times! I'm only kidding myself when I do that, though.

If you find that when you read, or write in a workbook, you are distracted by what's on the other page, try putting a blank sheet of paper over the page you're not using. It can help a lot and makes a good bookmark, too. Some books are printed on thin paper, so that the printing on the next page shows through. A piece of black paper *under* the page you're reading or working on cures that at once.

If you're distracted more by what you *hear* than what you *see*, you'll still need a tidy desk. (All that junk rattling around can be noisy.) And *turn off* the radio or stereo or TV if you find yourself listening to it and letting your homework just sit there. This is pretty hard to do—you're going to have to be pretty honest with yourself!

A good way to encourage yourself to do your homework or study without getting distracted so much is to reward yourself for your work. Instead of having a snack or watching a little TV *before* studying, try it this way.

Try to decide about how long each item on your list of homework or your studying ought to take. If math should take about 20 minutes, then promise yourself a reward when it's done, and give yourself just that much time. (A little kitchen timer that rings when time is up is even better than an alarm clock!) It's easier to work fast and well if you know ahead of time that it won't last forever—especially if there's a tall glass of milk and two chocolate-chip cookies at the end of the struggle!

If you're on a diet, your reward might be a five-minute bike ride or listening to one number on your favorite rock station for every 15 or 20 minutes of studying.

If you can work for a long time without tiring, how about an hour of TV for completing all your homework in a given time? Your parents will probably be only too glad to help out on the deal. Perhaps they'll be your timekeepers, or look over your completed homework. It's worth a try—and they may learn a method that'll work for your brothers and sisters, too.

Lots of people *without* learning disabilities have trouble remembering things; but it can be a special problem if you have a learning disability. You have already learned in Chapter 4 that if you're a visual learner, you remember things better if you *see* them. Auditory learners remember things better if they *hear* them. Here are a couple of memory boosters that might help, whichever way you learn best.

I'm sure you have heard people say, "Tie a string around your finger so you won't forget!" What they mean is, give yourself some physical hints to remind you that there is something you need to remember.

Suppose you have trouble remembering to take your gym clothes to school on Mondays. A way to help you remember is, on Sunday night, to hang them in their duffel bag on your bedroom doorknob so that you'll actually *touch* them when you go to open the door; or, if you roll them in a towel instead of using a duffel bag, prop them against the door so that they'll fall on your feet when you open the door.

You can use "doorknob reminders" any time there's something special you need to take to school or to do. Just taping a note on a much-used doorknob (your bedroom door, or perhaps the bathroom door) so that your hand will contact the paper as soon as you open the door will help.

I use a form of this same kind of reminder often. I used to have a dead car battery often on rainy or foggy days. I'd turn on the lights, and forget to turn them off when I got to work! (I'll bet your mom or dad has done the same thing.) Now, whenever I turn on my car lights during the daytime, I hang my floppy key chain over the top of the car key. That way, as soon as I start to turn off the engine, my fingers hit that key chain first, and I'm reminded. It's saved me lots of time–and teasing!

You might try some variations of this idea. It just might be the answer for you!

Another problem many kids with learning disabilities have is getting all worked up over small things. One minute, you're "happy as a clam"; and the next minute, you feel like it's the end of the world.

One thing that helps is just plain knowing that for you, that's normal. You've probably seen a two-year-old have a temper tantrum, and heard his parents say, "It's just a phase he's going through." Maybe if you can look at some of your moods this same way, they won't bug you so much. When you find yourself getting all worked up, or find that you just yelled at somebody over nothing at all, let yourself know, "There I go again. It's just a phase. In five minutes I'll be OK again."

That doesn't mean you shouldn't try to keep a lid on things–that *has* to be your responsibility, because nobody can do it but you. You know how "freaked out" you get when somebody else is putting the pressure on you!

And for Pete's sake, get plenty of sleep! Some people seem to need only a few hours sleep. Others are cross as bears without ten or twelve hours. Let your own body's reaction guide you and your parents to picking your bedtime. You may decide that 8:30's your bedtime, even if your kid brother stays up until 9:00.

Maybe some of these ideas will work for you. If you have some other problems that bug you, that you'd like to do something about, your teacher or counselor may be able to help you come up with some ideas you can try. The main thing is knowing that *you* can help *yourself*.

Chapter 6

"I've Got People Problems, Too!"

After you've gone through the big hassle of finding out about yourself and facing up to your problem (which wasn't as bad as all the things you imagined it could be!), you still have to face the problems that other people can cause you.

Sometimes people can cause you problems when they're really trying to help, but they just don't understand. Often, they think they know what the problem is, but they've got the wrong answer—just like you did, when you thought you were dumb!

You get tired of hearing people say that you don't try or that you don't care. You're sick of people blaming you for something that's not your fault, or blaming your parents, as though you were a "bad kid" and you and they were both to blame. And the people who go overboard the other way, thinking you're not as smart as you really are, are a *real* pain.

Maybe you can strike a blow for yourself and lots of other kids with learning disabilities, too, if you can educate these people. You've already started educating the most important one—yourself. Now let's see what you can do with the rest of the world!

Why not start with the ones who really care about you, but who can't always understand what it's like to be smart but to have trouble learning—your own parents.

I'm going to share some of my "trade secrets" with you. I travel around the country doing a special workshop for parents, or for teachers, that helps them understand what a learning disability feels like. I use games and tricks to make easy things hard for them; and I'm going to teach you how to use some of my sneaky tricks (but not all of them—I've got to have *some* secrets!) to help your parents, or your teachers, or even some of your friends see what learning with a learning disability feels like.

Here's a good one that I learned as a party game—guaranteed to frustrate dads, especially.

Draw a simple design on a piece of paper. (A dollar sign is a good one, but you can make any design that doesn't have mostly straight lines. Even just a random scrawl will work great.) Cover the design with a piece of tracing paper, and put a mirror on the table, so that your dad can see the design in the mirror. Then hold a piece of cardboard in front of him so that he *can't* see the paper, except in the mirror. Now ask him to trace the design.

He's in for quite a surprise! He'll be able to see the design, and know where he wants the pencil to go, but he'll have a hard time doing it. It will be as hard for him as learning to write is for some kids with learning problems. Maybe it will be easier for him to see why some of your papers are pretty messy!

This next stunt works best if you can type, or if you can get someone to type for you. (Pencil and paper will work, but not quite as well.) Take one piece of white paper and a piece of carbon paper. Put the carbon paper *under* the plain paper so that the carbon side is against the plain paper. Now type (or print carefully) a simple story on the front of the plain paper. (You can make up your own story, but it's easier to copy one from a book or magazine.) Now take the carbon paper away and look at the *back* of the story. It should look like this

!ʇɥɓᴉɹ ʇᴉ bᴉb noʎ ʇᴉ

Now, ask your parents or teacher if reading is easy! For some kids with learning disabilities, some or all of the letters may seem to get turned around that way. Maybe it was like that for you.

Another reading trick is to copy a long paragraph or a story, putting in X's instead of vowels.

Xt lxxks lxkx thxs.

Try this out on your "victims." You can probably think of lots of ways to show reading problems—just having them read a story with the *d*'s, *p*'s, *b*'s, *g*'s, and *q*'s all switched around is great fun!

You can try a math game, too. Tell your "victim" that you are going to change the rules for math. Say that the "+" sign means subtract, the "÷" sign means multiply, the "−" sign means divide, and the "x" sign means add. Then write a long, *easy* problem down for him to work, like:

$$6 + 2 \div 1 \ x \ 4 - 2 =$$

Bet he can't get the right answer! (I *think* the answer is 4, but I've even confused myself!)

These are good activities for helping people understand learning disabilities. Sometimes in my workshops I have had parents really understand their son's or daughter's problem for the first time. One father had talked to me for a long time. He felt his son, Larry, just didn't try hard enough, and that "learning disability" was just an excuse. He loved his son, but he just couldn't see why this very smart boy had so much trouble learning. The man finally tried the mirror drawing trick. He worked and worked: he smudged the paper, broke the pencil (and I think he may even have said one or two words he shouldn't have); and when he "finished," you couldn't even recognize the design. He looked at it for a very long time, and shook his head. He seemed to be talking to himself when he said, very quietly, "Don't yell at Larry, don't yell at Larry."

If it helped Larry, maybe it'll help you, too.

That's about it. Now you know what your problems are, how to work around them, and how to help people understand you better. Your part of this book is just about finished! The next chapter may be a special treat, though. It will give you lots of "homework"—but not to do, yourself. It's homework to assign to your parents and teachers! You can look the list over and pick out things you think they need to find out about . . . or just turn the whole job over to them.

Chapter 7

Work To Assign Your Parents And Teachers

Well, why not? Your teachers give you assignments at school, and your parents give you chores to do at home. Now you can assign *them* a little "homework." Assign the rest of this chapter to them—and your work is over!

First, there are some organizations parents and teachers might consider joining.

Association for Children with Learning Disabilities (ACLD)
5225 Grace Street
Pittsburgh, PA   15236

This group is for both parents and teachers, as well as other people concerned about learning disabilities. They have local groups all over the country, so if parents write to this address, they can get the address of the group nearest them. There are great newsletters, with news about TV shows about learning disabilities, movies, books, legislation, and meetings. Many local groups have newsletters, too, and some have "lending libraries" that would have many of the books I'm going to suggest later. (Don't let the word "children" in the name fool you—they're interested in teenagers, too.)

Council for Exceptional Children (CEC), and its
Division for Children with Learning Disabilities (DCLD)
1920 Association Drive
Reston, VA   22091

This is mainly a group for teachers and other professionals working with youngsters with all kinds of special needs (the gifted, the retarded, the physically handicapped—as well as the learning disabled.) The DCLD is a special group for learning disabilities. CEC has two journals its members receive, as well as newsletters. DCLD has a newsletter, and a new journal.

There are several journals that teachers and parents have found very useful. Each of these journals has a slightly different purpose. Parents and teachers might find that different ones suit each of them best.

Academic Therapy
P.O. Box 899
20 Commercial Blvd.
Novato, CA 94947

This journal comes out five times a year. It has articles for teachers and for parents on all sorts of topics having to do with learning disabilities. There are lots of "how-to" articles here! There are also book reviews and information on new teaching materials.

Journal of Learning Disabilities
101 East Ontario Street
Chicago, IL 60611

This journal comes out monthly, October through May, with June/July and August/September, which are combined. There are more teacher-oriented and research-type articles in this journal, but an occasional article of special interest to parents. There are book reviews and information about new materials, too.

The Exceptional Parent
Room 708, Statler Office Building
20 Providence Street
Boston, MA 02116

This is a special magazine just for parents of children with special problems, not just learning disabilities, but also for children with major handicaps. The magazine keeps parents up to date on the law, materials, sources of help and information, and how other parents have helped their children handle problems.

Two organizations which can provide very good lists of reading materials, and from whom many inexpensive books and pamphlets can be ordered, are ACLD (address above) and CANHC:

California Association for Neurologically Handicapped Children
PO Box 604 Main Office
Los Angeles, CA   90053

You can also get many inexpensive paperback books (some are listed later) and materials from Academic Therapy Publications (address also above). Now for some important reading!

First, here are some major books on learning disabilities. I have tried to give some idea of the orientation of each book to help you select according to what you want from the book. This is by no means a complete list, but you will find that each book in this survey will lead you to several others.

Children with Learning Disabilities by Janet W. Lerner (Boston: Houghton-Mifflin Company, 1971).

This book is subtitled "Theories, Diagnosis, and Teaching Strategies"; and it really does cover all of that! It also features several extremely useful appendices: one on phonics; one on sources of materials, with lists and brief descriptions of types of materials, information about types of tests; a list of publishers (and their addresses); and a glossary of learning disability terms used in the book.

Learning Disabilities: Educational Principles and Practices by Doris J. Johnson and Helmer R. Myklebust (New York: Grune and Stratton, 1967).

This textbook covers a great deal of material, related to specific learning problems. The orientation is psychoneurological, and there are remedial activities of many types included.

Educating Children with Learning Disabilities: Selected Readings edited by Edward C. Frierson and Walter B. Barbe (New York: Appleton-Century-Crofts, 1967).

This book provides an excellent sampler of ideas from many of the established experts in the field of learning disabilities.

Educational Perspectives in Learning Disability edited by Donald D. Hammill and Nettie R. Bartel (New York: John Wiley & Sons, Inc., 1971).

This is another good sampler. You'll see where the experts

stand, and will probably find some whose writings you'll want to see more of.

Directory of Facilities for the Learning-Disabled and Handicapped by Careth Ellingson and James Cass (New York: Harper & Row, 1972).

With this book, you can locate special schools and diagnostic facilities all over the United States and Canada. Information about staff, individual programs, special services, and costs (at the time of publication) are also given.

This next list contains books which are primarily oriented towards *teaching* the child with learning disabilities, especially special methods to use. Some are useful to parents for special help at home, too.

Methods for Learning Disorders by Patricia I. Myers and Donald D. Hammill (New York: John Wiley & Sons, Inc., 1969).

For an excellent review of some of the major theorists and their methods, this book is superb.

Teaching Children with Learning Problems by Gerald Wallace and James M. Kauffman (Columbus, Ohio: Charles E. Merrill Publishing Co., 1973).

This book adopts a behavior modification approach to learning problems, but also supplies an extensive guide to teaching activities designed to work on specific learning areas.

Aids to Psycholinguistic Teaching by Wilma Jo Bush and Marian Taylor Giles (Columbus, Ohio: Charles E. Merrill Publishing Co., 1969).

This is a very practical book of remedial activities, divided by grade level and by type of learning problem as diagnosed by the *Illinois Test of Psycholinguistic Abilities*. There's only a sentence or two of theory per chapter—the rest of the book is filled with activities.

Activities for Developing Visual Perception by Polly Behrmann (San Rafael, California: Academic Therapy Publications, 1970).

This little paperback has dozens of activities that are useful for children with visual perception problems but fun for all.

Education as Therapy by Ruth Mallison (Seattle: Special Child Publications, 1968).

Each chapter in this paperback is a response to a question about the educational program. The emphasis is on neurological handicap.

How Many Spoons Make a Family? by Polly Behrmann and Joan Millman (San Rafael, California: Academic Therapy Publications, 1971).

This is a family-oriented paperback of math games and simple home activities which can be used with school-age and preschool normal as well as learning-disabled children. Teachers will be able to adapt many of the activities to the classroom.

Learning Problems in the Classroom by Marianne Frostig and Phyllis Maslow (New York: Grune & Stratton, Inc., 1973).

After a theoretical background, this book moves into preventive and remedial activities. Those who are familiar with the pencil-and-paper Frostig materials for visual perception will find these activities much more inclusive, covering a wider range of problems.

A Special Way for the Special Child in the Regular Classroom by Patricia Murphy (San Rafael, California: Academic Therapy Publications, 1971).

Regular classroom teachers will find this book a useful collection of remedial activities which can be done in the classroom. Also included are lists of appropriate tests and materials.

Teaching Through Sensory-Motor Experiences edited by John I. Arena (San Rafael, California: Academic Therapy Publications, 1969).

Many practical activities as well as well-presented theoretical materials are included in this book of readings.

The Teacher's Guide to the Brain and Learning by Max Schnitker, MD (San Rafael, California: Academic Therapy Publications, 1972).

For teachers (and parents) who've sought an easy-to-understand book on the brain, this paperback is the answer. It includes not only basic brain functioning, but a review of a number of theories on learning.

Teacher Diagnosis of Educational Difficulties by Robert M. Smith (Columbus, Ohio: Charles E. Merrill Publishing Company, 1969).

This is an excellent text aimed at helping teachers do informal classroom diagnosis of academic problems. The goal is to develop strategies for solutions, not merely to define problems.

In Chapter 5, the reader learned how to make studying easier and more efficient by providing rewards for himself or herself for completion of set amounts of work. This is a form of *behavior modification*, a method which emphasizes the "carrot" rather than the "stick"! Parents and teachers both may find these books, most of which are available in paperback, good sources for step-by-step instruction in this method.

Living with Children by Gerald R. Patterson and M. Elizabeth Gullion (Champaign, Illinois: Research Press, 1968).

This is a self-teaching "programed" book, easy to use and understand.

Parents are Teachers by Wesley C. Becker (Champaign, Illinois: Research Press, 1971).

This book is similar to *Living with Children*, but perhaps more complete. The examples make it easy to understand the principles discussed.

You Can Help Your Child Improve Study and Homework Behaviors by Steven M. Zifferblatt (Champaign, Illinois: Research Press, 1970).

This book teaches the method of behavior modification by concentrating specifically on homework and study problems.

My Mom Uses Behavior Modification by Thelma D. White (Grove City, Ohio: South-Western City Schools, 1972).

This is both a description of a school district's parent-training project (with guidelines for setting up such a program), and an instructional manual for parents.

Changing Children's Behavior by John D. Krumboltz and Helen Brandhorst Krumboltz (Englewood Cliffs, New Jersey: Prentice-Hall, Inc., 1972).

This is an excellent book on behavior modification, and includes a number of techniques and solutions to problems not discussed in many other books on this method.

No teacher or parent can be expected to rush out and join all these groups or read all these books. Each contact made, and each book read, however, will be a further step toward the knowledge and understanding needed to help the child whose problem led them to this book, and to helping all children.